I

c

o

p

e

THERE SHOULD BE FLOWERS

JOSHUA JENNIFER ESPINOZA

Poems in this collection have appeared in one form or another in *Alice Blue Review, Apogee Journal, The Feminist Wire, HOAX, Nepantla, The Offing, PEN America, Potluck Mag, Shabby Doll House, Vetch,* and *Washington Square Review.*

IT IS IMPORTANT TO BE SOMETHING

This is like a life. This is lifelike.
I climb inside a mistake
and remake myself in the shape
of a better mistake—
a nice pair of glasses
without any lenses,
shoes that don't quite fit,
a chest that always hurts.
There is a checklist of things
you need to do to be a person.
I don't want to be a person
but there isn't a choice,
so I work my way down and
kiss the feet.
I work my way up and lick
the knee.
I give you my skull
to do with whatever you please.
You grow flowers from my head
and trim them too short.
I paint my nails nice and pretty
and who cares. Who gives a shit.
I'm trying not to give a shit
but it doesn't fit well on me.
I wear my clothes. I wear my body.
I walk out in the grass and turn red
at the sight of everything.

I DREAM OF HORSES EATING COPS

I dream of horses eating cops
I have so much hope for the future

or no I don't

Who knows the sound a head makes when it is asleep
My dad was a demon but so was the white man in uniform
who harassed him for the crime of being brown

There are demons everywhere
dad said
and he was right but not in the way he meant it

The sky over San Bernardino was a brilliant blue when the winds kicked in
All the fences and trash cans and smog scattered themselves
and the mountains were on fire every day

I couldn't wait to die or be killed
my woman body trapped in a dream

I couldn't wait to wake up
and ride off into the sunset
but there isn't much that's new anywhere

The same violence swallows itself and produces bodies
and names for bodies

I name my body girl of my dreams
I name my body proximity
I name my body full of hope despite everything
I name my body dead girl who hasn't died yet

I hope I come back as an elephant
I hope we all come back as animals
and eat our fill

I hope everyone gets everything they deserve

THERE SHOULD BE FLOWERS

There should be more to life
than disruption
and survival
but there isn't.
There should be birds
singing your name.
There should be paintings
the size of skyscrapers
memorializing your body.
There should be love
for you
in everything.
There should be a billion women
jumping at the same time
to move the earth off its course.
There should be parties
to celebrate
the end of this world.
There should be flowers
to welcome
a new one.

THE COUNTERPUBLIC WOMEN

I teeth. I crawl. The heart

beats slowly. There is always time.

You smell smoke. You are creeped

out. I die. I die. I lick the door handle and die

from the taste of it.

We are in a house together feeling the walls.

Feeling the air on the carpet.

You breathe onto my tongue. I smell smoke.

Nothing strange. Nothing unusual.

My body haha. Your body haha.

Who'd've thought. Who'd've cared.

My hair is streaked with hours.

I walk out into the wind and think of you

standing in the wind. How you feel yourself.

Your little lips. This kind of social. This kind of forest fire.

I am only gone from you whenever I sleep, and

I wake up sad. There is so much loss in sleep.

The sky is pink in sleep.

The skin is enlarged in sleep.

Every dream is a dream about having a body.

Every body is the sound of alienation.

AUTOPAINOPHILE

My favorite thing is slowly pulling
into my parking spot at home
just as the song I've been feeling
things to finally ends.

All these movie moments and
hand cutting wind in half dreams
come for me as if
sent by some light that wants
to watch me survive.

In the movies people like me
don't survive and it's the same
in real life so I make my own
movies in my head and I last
til the end and I am not
happy even in my own
fantasy but I am strong.

I am holding the camera and
pointing it at myself so I am
trapped in my own gaze
which is fine
which feels great
which is like the taste of my
own blood
which is great.

I wish I loved my body the
way you say I love my body and
I wish the sun would stay just
below the horizon forever.

I'M IN A LOVE/HATE RELATIONSHIP WITH HAVING A BODY

I'm in a love/hate relationship
with having a body.

I'm in a relationship with having a body
and it's complicated.

I'm in a long distance relationship
with having a body.

I try to imagine existing
in a body that makes sense.

What if my body became a cloud,
I'm always thinking.

Instead I sit on the couch
and switch my gaze back and forth
from screen to sky
until I feel like I've accomplished something great.

There should be awards given out
for things like showering, going to the grocery store,
and breathing,
but no one cares. I care. Lots of people care
but ultimately no one cares.

Sometimes I text my body little hearts
from outer space
and she laughs and I can hear her
from all the way up here.

Sometimes I think I'm going to die
and then I remember that I definitely am
going to die.

I hope I come back as a tree,
stay alive for a thousand years,
and never have to think about anything.

I IMAGINE ALL MY CIS FRIENDS LAUGHING AT TRANNY JOKES

I imagine all my cis friends laughing at tranny jokes
whenever I'm not around. I can hear the sound of rain
outside and I'm grasping for the words to say this. There
is nothing I love more than an honest storm. Broken dishes.
Dead grass. The time has come for me to be alive
and for you to stop speaking. Please stop speaking. Please, oh
please stop speaking. I have never felt as alone as this,
I say every day. I have never felt so alone. I've built houses
in corners of houses and filled them with all of my
longings. My strength. My pride. My beauty. My woman
self. I read another comments section of an article
about trans women and I want to die. To not exist. To let
them win. I don't let them win. I circle the drain
and kiss my fingers hello. I welcome them back. This complex
trauma responds only to the dialectical. Only to the heat
and the cool, the death and the life. Only then is it lifted
for a moment to let me breathe. I breathe the sweet air
and stare at the hillside, and then at the road, and then
at the cars, and then at the sky. All so unsure of themselves.
All so softly shaking in place. All so beautifully living.

COMFORT

11 am. Time to wake up.

Muscles sore, jaw clenched, warm light

scattering dreams of violence across

the bedroom. I've chosen a self

too large for this body. Too willing to

change for others. Too beautiful

to appear in public. I'd tell you to walk

in my feet but they're all I have left.

I've been weathered down to the

ankles by all the news reports. All the

listening. All the not doing.

When I crawl out of bed I don't

know where to go. What to say.

I tried to talk about comfort

but how do you describe a color

you've never been allowed to see?

TRAPPED IN MY BODY I DREAM

Wrapped in my body I dream
of being something else

outside of time, space, energy,
love, death, gender, capitalism,

etc. Who could lift such a weight?
Not me. I am one thing, after all,

sucking on its own poisons.
The idea I could or should be

beautiful. The song of songs
that sings itself to sleep.

The thought of heaven
without a hell.

The whisper of life
without a death.

The dream of salvation
without blood.

MY FIRST LOVE

My first love was silence.
I built myself from scratch
and no one listened.
This was the best time of my life.
I used to carry the clothes
to the laundry room
and pray for all the fog
in the world to surround me.
I'd let my thoughts
catch rides
with the passing planes.
All that womanhood
caught in the roof
of my mouth
was like honey.
I knew it would never
go bad
so I never said a word
about it.

WHEN THE SONG SLOWS DOWN

When the song slows down
I come in and take a break
from the too muchness of outside
the heavy movement of things
the radio static I can still hear
when I'm halfway to the door.
Paint a sunroof on my head
so I can see what a ceiling looks like.
Break the glass
so I can watch a sky unoccupied
with thoughts.
Oh god, this is a dream
this is all a dream
I once had about walking out into
the living room to find
trees, bushes, dirt, rocks
scattered and growing
through the ground and the walls.
Years later I'd still sometimes forget
this didn't actually happen
that my body didn't climb out of
itself and smile at what it saw
unencumbered
by skin and feeling.

I AM DRAPED IN HEAVENLY SKIN

I am draped in heavenly skin
from head to toe. Back then they said

you could never be the girl you know
yourself to be. I knew too much

about myself to stay alive. I stayed
alive. I wrote names on my body with

pins, nails, knives, fire, anything
that would mark the flesh.

This kind of violence is a shrine
to itself. The way it touches you

without breathing, thinking, feeling.
What is left of me? The songs I sang

to keep from sleeping sound like
nothing more than rain. I woke up

this morning a garden. I took pictures
of all my flowers. I was beautiful

as far as I could tell.

THIS IS A POEM ABOUT THE POWER OF POSITIVE THINKING

This is a poem about the power of positive thinking.

I cry into my hands.

I cry into my pillow.

I dedicate whole afternoons to feeling my emotions

in a healthy way.

I drink so much water.

I walk next to the freeway and down the hill.

Someone shouts "you're ugly".

Dogs bark at the sunset.

All these eighties movie houses drown

in purple light.

Back at home I think I feel an earthquake.

I remember all the women who haven't made it.

I think about not making it.

I don't watch the news

or google my symptoms

but then I get bored and I watch the news

and I google my symptoms.

I wrap myself in dirty sheets

and smoke a bowl

and drink a glass.

I avoid the mirror again

and then I look in the mirror for

what feels like two minutes but

is closer to an hour.

Where is the song? The beauty? The movement? The playfulness? The life?

I am nowhere to be found in myself

because I am so good at hiding.

I hid for fifteen years

and then for another eight years after that.

I fell in love with the quiet disjointed rhythms

of commanding the wrong body

the wrong voice

the wrong name.

There is so much I have left to give you

but now I want it all for myself.

TRAN

There are so many things—

The swell before she says it
a lifetime of air
vacuumed
exposed to the empty
sound of caring

All the space inside it
before her tongue unfurls
before her teeth
clap together

The dust
and city lights
freewayed through her chest

Screaming woman
trans woman
trans woman
trans woman
tranny tran tran tran

Anything but the breath
held in any longer

Anything but the blood
sitting still in her heart

All that bending light
forming words
to handcuff her to existence

All that sorrow
at the discovery
of her name
carved into an old coffee table
left next to a dumpster

Her broken glass
still consistent in its longings
slicing the air in half
to bring her some beauty

THIS POEM IS A PERSONAL ESSAY

This poem is a personal essay.
I love to feel crowded
by the leaves in my hands
and the birds in my mouth.
There is so much time
for me to get better.
No there isn't.
I've only ever seen the sky
open once
and I didn't get to kiss it.
I always want to say "who cares"
when I mean to say "I care".
This is not my only flaw.
In the shower
a universe slides off me
and five more take its place.

I DON'T KNOW HOW TO TELL YOU THIS

I don't know how to tell you this
but I'm ten leaves floating
in a pool of rainwater
that you hop over on your way
to work every day.
I was hoping I would live
long enough to see your gaze
catch my gaze
but this is the way things are.
The sun is out and people are happy.
Bodies perform labor and people are happy.
Trans women die and people are happy.
Everything is so happy.
It feels good to close your eyes
and dance with a breeze
on a cool spring day
doesn't it? God, how those simple
pleasures mean so much.
No pleasure is that simple for me.
Each one is a stone
held in place
just below the surface of some ocean.
I leap
from one to another
hoping this won't be the time I drown.

LIKE A GOOD WOMAN

Like a good woman
I apologize.
We are all approximations
of what we are.
I said I would never again be
anyone's crumbs
but here I am
eating dust and late
afternoon sunlight
for your amusement.
I won't say anything
else about it.
There are trees outside
my window
filled with dozens
of hummingbirds.
I want to offer them
the sugar from my tongue
because they would never
think to ask for it.

THE PUBLIC REACHES

The public reaches into my head

and drops rocks, leaves, tow trucks,

old white ladies who stare, grocery stores,

cracked freeways, the sight of these mountains

from an angle I hadn't seen before,

bobcats, hummingbirds, coyotes, a clocktower,

a patch of new grass, people walking

around each other, the sound of a door slamming

that reminds me of the beginning of an

earthquake, the beginning of an earthquake,

a bright light in the sky I can't explain,

a gathering of clouds,

a low rumble,

a cashier who calls me "sir", a tornado

over the road, a truck flipped on its side,

all the dust in the world, all the dust that has

ever existed, everything in my body that screams "wrong",

sunlight, sunlight, so much sunlight

pouring down through the window

and onto the carpet where I wait inside

for all of this to end.

SOFT HELL

I'm just a small town tran
living in a soft hell
where rocks reach for clouds
and people are doing their best.
Everyone is doing their best everywhere.
This is the most depressing fact of life.
When you clung to yourself
outside in the parking lot
amongst the vomit and broken glass
did I say anything? No
I just loved
and loved
and loved and loved and loved
until my body drained
into the gutter
where the rain from years had gathered
to watch true change.
I emerged from myself
like a woman caked in shit
her heart encased in amber
beating softly
feeling out the world
after millennia of sleep.
I wake up every morning and say "Thank god"
even though I'm no longer sure
she actually exists.

WHO SHE WAS

She said who she was
with all that happened to her.

They told her who she was
with what they did to her.

Make no mistake—
this sound is endless.

The legs she grew
from the seeds they planted
carry on and on and on
uncontained by any soil

any crime

any violent gesture
towards understanding.

She knows when she cries
for peace
she means someone else's
blood.

They know when they taste
her blood
that she was who she said she was—

what they said
when they were making her.

MY BODY A SIEVE

My body a sieve for gender.

My gender a habitat.

A plant growing sideways out of my belly

I write "hips" on.

Seeing is not knowing or even believing.

I have the all-seeing cock,

the girlish flesh I sharpen with my scissor fingers

and then turn inward on myself.

Every woman comes from blood

and lives in blood and dies in blood

her endless vines twitching below the canopy.

She lives where the sun is known

as possibility.

I am unknown to the sun

though it blesses me

with its warmth from time to time.

Even if I were with it

I could never look at it.

All our she-who-must-not-be-loved bodies

make a home in the dirt

learn to swallow the dirt

learn to move it through us like prayer.

After long enough it doesn't feel like anything.

After long enough I forget.

Nothing can be retained if I am to survive.

WIND POEM #1

I am saying I
and walking up some hillside
where my body becomes wind
and I love wind and I am so happy and sad.
I would live another year if for no other reason
than to feel it again.
I believe in ritual.
I listen to myself in the car with the window
halfway down. I imagine I'd fly out
and tumble down the road like a scrap of trash.
I'd be the cutest piece of trash in this city.
Instead I wash my hands and train my voice
to sound like soft gusts against cold glass.
I push a lawnmower over my chin.
I paint my face with white and red and white
and more white.
I draw black lines to highlight separation.
I pull my body inside out and fall in love
with the feeling of not dying.
All of this labor is like some kind of prayer
to prove I deserve to exist in these spaces
to prove I deserve to exist in space
to prove I deserve to exist.

WIND POEM #2

It is quiet in the morning.
I am female-bodied.
Last night's air is still
inside the trees.
A loud clap of thunder
from earlier this month
is stuck in the window.
I dress myself with
a large paper bag
and go outside in the wind.
Nothing happens.
I shudder
and break into pieces
but nothing happens.
You come out and find me
alone in the grass
covered in a purple rash.
You call me lacking
and kiss me with the words
that erase me from existence.
Everything I am
comes from a place of dying.

NATURE

I'm older than you realize. I've been
around for so long, you don't even
know. I've been lapping up rain
water since forever ago. Since you first
heard me coming, I'd been alive
a million years before that. I don't
stop coming. I never tie that garden
hose around my neck or swallow
that airplane. I kiss you. I forgive
you. No I don't, never mind. You're
lucky I'm so much this mirror for you
to hold. You're lucky I kiss so good.
You're lucky I don't put snake
venom in my lipstick first. Take us
both out. No, I just daydream and
tug on my girly dick until the sky
notices me. Did I say the right words?
Did you notice me? Do you love
how my body shakes when I
come for the last time ever? I can
see everything now, everything now,
everything now in front of me,
ceiling fans in the clouds, railroad
tracks in my fingers, bedroom full of
orange and brown leaves, the end
of the world at last.

NURTURE

A palm leaf twinges with guilt.   What is beneath
this machine?

A man walks through a door
and a woman climbs out a window.   What is being
described?

A strand of skin reaches out to kiss
everything it signifies.   Who is listening?

A body moves in time towards
all the violence it contains.   What is going
on?

Trash scatters itself
among more trash
and dares to give itself a name.   What is being
named?

A trans woman lies dead
in the middle of a street
her body a parade
for laughter, joy, and silence.   What is beneath
this machine?

ASSIGNED AT BIRTH

Socialized dead thing
crawls out of her clothing pile

She is nighttime on fire
        inside herself
It is safe inside
where shadows hold all feeling

and, still, shadowed
across the face
        she paints

What confusing signs
What communication
What a daydream

        they say

And what a miracle it is
    that they say
 anything at all

Her sideways heart speaks
about its situation and

it, the dream, seems so far
away from her

Here
in the sun suffering
the smell of her
        own sweat

The bitter hair
        clinging
to her face

All becomes too much to say

PERFORMANCE

Suffering to entertain cis
bodies/ bore my
        self to death

To death to self

Who eats, who draws blood
from the gums

Who eats, who doesn't eat

Who remembers
        not eating
in January
        and February
and December and March and July and noontime

Who drinks from the fridge
and collects quarters
for her body

*

The sound of reenactment:

ironed clothing
smell of burning clothing
on the iron

on the hot summer on the june

skin drying in the june

god remembers what
you've done

male-body'd on the hill/ plastic bayonet
sticking out   of her chest

round of applause from the audience
and, oh   here we go

SHE IMAGINES A FUTURE NOT UNLIKE THIS FUTURE

Please stop speaking. Please stop touching.
This is the end of the performance.

There is a myth that you will listen to
about your own body
that will map you into existence.

You will pour water on your face
and roll around in the dirt
for that natural look.

The idea is to create a self
through the destruction of another self
but it never works out that way.

You have a voice
but you can only use words
so you don't really have a voice.

I'm no longer interested in suffering as entertainment
meaning I'm no longer interested in entertainment
or suffering.

Empathy becomes something like a rash
that you give yourself
when you stand in front of the mirror
and think about resistance.

Your face shifts and bleeds into the walls
and what will your mouth do
apart from what mouths are meant to do
and what will your hands do
apart from what hands are meant to do.

GROWTH RITUAL

It's 10:00 am somewhere.
My uncles are children
blushing in the grass
unaware of who I've become.
I haven't heard god
whisper anything in my ear
in many years.
Not since I lived
in that old house and
slept in mom's old bedroom
where the sun baked
the wall against the bed.
I woke up every morning
with my head on fire,
one thousand panic attacks
a month,
dangling roots scattering dirt
all across the floor,
my body rebuilding itself
from the sky up.

HISTORY

The earth was cut open and drained of itself.

The sand poured out of me before my

body was more than a dream.

My white grandma said "send them all

back to Mexico where they belong".

It was almost too much for my heart to take

but my heart has learned to be

whatever it needs to be

to survive.

I can get through anything

if I change the shape of it enough.

This generational trauma

writes the poem for me.

The pain is inside the blood

and it forms the skin

and it tells the mind what to fear.

I fear everything

that exists and has ever existed

and will ever exist.

I FORGOT WHERE I WAS

I forgot where I was.
It was June 1st
and the air was dying.
I had empathy for the dirt
as it consumed
the grass.
I played games on my phone
until the world became
a fogged up window.
Where was I again.
The body, yes. The body.
It moves like nothing else
ever has.
Something in you had to die
before you could
inhabit your body.
I can feel what it is
when I wake up sober
for the first time in a month.
Dreams are always tainted
by ideas of what dreams
should be.
Don't tell me anything.
I'm here. I'm here. I exist.
Thank god I remember
how small I am.

IN THE MEN'S GROUP

In the men's group at church
I felt like a spy. Dad had forced me
to go with him in what seemed
like a last ditch attempt to fill me
with god and masculinity.
They sat in rows of plastic
fold out chairs and listened to
the tallest white guy in the room
speak about what it meant to be a man.
He recounted going out
to dinner with his wife and
lamented over the pink-haired queer
who served them their food.
When he made fun of the queer's
lisp all the men laughed
and secretly prayed for god
to be as cruel as they were.

I didn't laugh. I was beyond
pretending. I was cutting my wrists
inside my mind and bleeding out
in front of all those fuckers.
Afterwards I silently drank water
from a wax cup while dad introduced
me around. He paused awkwardly as
he said, "This is my son".

I think he knew.
I think they all knew I wasn't one of them.
I think god died in me that morning
and came back to life a woman
with long hair and a five o'clock
shadow that just wouldn't quit.
When I prayed for the very last time
I told her my true name and she just
listened. She didn't laugh.
Years later when I came out to dad
he said, "I know. I've known."

BODY'D

Those summers I was
a soft bitch
dripping with teeth.

I drank nail polish
from a mug
and let you flip my
body over.

There was a cloud
on the edge of
the cliff we lived on.

I let you flip
my body over
into the shadow
of a tree.

I never talked
to anyone
on the internet about
my body.
I was dying

in my body.
I never
dreamed of electric

blue light licking
my soft
bitch skin

while you pounded
it in like waves.

MOAT

In a dream I called you
and hung up as soon as I heard your voice

My body has healed now
It is a twenty story building
made of rocks and trees and ivy

There is so much left of me
to give to the earth
and to deny you

So I will end here
where I am happy
and quietly falling
out of your memory

GODDAMN THIS POEM

Goddamn this poem
is like pulling teeth
Like finding the perfect tooth
in a pile of teeth
Like hills of dust and teeth
formed by a million years
of grinding teeth
Like yellow teeth
Like white shining teeth
Like blood red teeth
Like the whisper of air
moving between teeth
Like a sky made of teeth
full of clouds made of teeth
gnashing and chewing
and biting at the air
which is also teeth
Like teeth teething
at the empty spaces
between the tiniest particles
little teeth spinning
and dizzying
and working
to form something bigger
something fraught
with too much meaning
Like words made of teeth
    a language of teeth
coming to life and dying
inside a single breath.

FOREST FIRE

I'm a fire in the rain

or maybe I'm the rain
trying to put out the fire
with no luck

Maybe I'm the fog
that surrounds
the trees that are on fire

Maybe I'm the trees
that are on fire

Maybe I'm the fawn
caught in the fire
surrounded by rain
and fog
and trees

Maybe I'm the dream
the fawn has
as it suffocates quietly
inside the smoke
of the fire

Maybe I'm the fire
when it first starts
but then I become the rain
and then the fog
and then the trees
and then the fawn
and then the dream

Maybe I am nothing
after all

WHAT I AM GIVEN

Apologies

Hailstorms of kindness

Small drop of kindness

to suckle

from the death thing

My mother calls me and I don't answer

The sky opens

and I answer

How will I find love for myself

in myself

I am all out of room and have been

for many years

I've never kept a diary

because I want to forget everything

YOU ARE A TREE IN YOURSELF

You are a tree in yourself in your garden.

The world calls the dream of your body
into question.

Your skin gets drawn out
over the muscle of the sky.

Feelings come to remind you
that you might exist.

When you cry you are saying I love you
to yourself

but there is history.
There is time.
there are forces at work

in your chest
and in your room, and in your house,
and in your public,

and in the looks on the faces of those
who narrate your body
when they see you.

So much is leaving you when you give
yourself to the world.

When you walk,
the ground seems to breathe you out.

THIS SUNSET IS SO BEAUTIFUL

This sunset is so beautiful I want
to be fucked by it.
I identify as the earth
and as everything
that has ever happened to me.
I'd swear on my name
all of it is true
but I don't have one. Not yet.
This sound I make waking up
is too young
still full of sadness
at all I am waiting for.
They called me a girl
when I was a girl
and when I became a woman
they said no. You can't do that.
I can do whatever I want
except drive on freeways
walk alone at night
or love myself.
A warm light grabs me by the wrist
and says listen. Listen.
You can forget everything. You can
start new somewhere else.
I start new somewhere else
every time I breathe,
I reply.

THIS CONFESSION IS A TREE

All of me points sideways

at the wall, at the curb, at the starlit

summer nights I spent waiting

to become this woman.

So much has happened I can't even begin.

I painted myself on ceilings

and let people pull off chunks of me

and name them whatever.

The outside air was a dream.

I took many blows

many blows

many blows

and now the kiss of wind is

almost too much.

This confession is a tree.

Please hold it gently

against me

while I breathe.

UNTITLED

There is a crease in what I say
when I say I am a woman.
There is a sound that ricochets
off the sound of my voice
holding itself down.
There is a barrier between my tongue
and my teeth
where who I am lives
waiting for the right words to come.
No words are right.
I am in the sky saying birds
when I mean the thing that birds do
to make the sky more beautiful.
I am that—
not the sight or the sound or the feeling
but the absence
of what was there before.

AFFIRMATIONS

I grasp at straws to breathe through
all that is inside the wind.
My body is inside the wind tugging
on herself
smearing lipstick up and down her face
tucking secrets behind her ears
like loose strands of hair.
I am caught up in the sight of myself.
What is happening to me.
Panic has replaced my blood today.
I say "I am going to stand up
and walk into the kitchen"
and then I stand up and walk into the kitchen.
This is the best I can do for now.
I stare out the window at the trees that move
and the pollen that swirls all around
and I forget what the word "life" means.
I am alive in myself
born to birds
who spoke a language
that never fit me.
So I say girl.
So I say woman.
So I say body.
None of it makes sense
but this is the best I can do for now.

NO MAN

Warm light floods everything you see.
I've been my own savior
out of necessity
for most of this life
storing my womanhood
beneath trees
to be forgotten
by everyone but me.
I no longer believe in the individual
or community.
I believe only in cause and effect.
Some great energy
pulls me here and there.
Some power smacks me around.
Some wind pushes us together
and we do the best we can
to breathe.
I've been waiting for the big earthquake
to come rip California
away from everything else.
They say no man is an island
but I am no man.
I am mountains and sand and sand and
so much sand
coming together for one moment
to know myself
before drifting away
towards something else.

MEN IN BODIES

Men in bodies make sounds
that last a lifetime.

Women in clouds gather
around the destruction
and sing.

Everything is alive in her
suffering. No meaning
to it at all.

I am her
because I do this
and the only thing I love

is listening
or becoming

all of her in my back
carrying me away
from this.

THE WOMAN IS ABOUT HAIR

The woman is about hair
gathering on the ground and between the breasts
that move up and down with each breath
in suffering.

In twenty years I will exist.
Even if I'm dead in twenty years I will exist
more than I do now.

I shave my legs in the shower
until my ass goes numb.

The water gathers all of me around
and says "that's what you get"
the same way men say
"that's just how the world works"
as if they're happy about it.

I make a prayer for you in front of the closet mirror
where the light from inside moves
around the room to see itself reflected.

The woman sees herself in everything and nothing.

You can open the news and read
anything you want to.

That's the magic of being alive here.

You can even read about yourself
long after you're dead.

SALT

When I thought of my body I saw a desert

covered in teeth marks.

I've had to let go of so many things

to get here.

The first time I called myself a girl

was when you called me a girl.

Nothing is unrelated.

Even the way I move from bedroom to kitchen

and from calm to panicked

makes sense in its own way.

You ask me for my name

and I dip my body in blue nail polish

and roll across the sidewalk.

It is warm

and I think of how birth and death

have become confused in my mind.

I know where I come from.

You don't need to remind me.

I've covered it all in salt

so I'll never forget.

US

The world pits us against one another

like soft lights

sent flickering across a room

to swallow more light

This is horrific

the sound it makes when

we feel too much

next to each other

Please, you know my poison

and I know your poison

I'll read your lips if I have to

I'll take your pulse

and tell you everything is going to be fine

even though it won't be

and you'll live through the earthquake

and I'll survive the flood

and we'll be a faint purple glow

at the end of it all

IT WAS SUPPOSED TO RAIN

It was supposed to rain today
I was supposed to be born a girl
There were supposed to be people
who loved you
for the simple fact that you exist

There were supposed to be flash floods
in my hometown
down the street from my old house

Language was supposed to save us

We were all supposed to be flesh
without name

There was supposed to be a chance of thunder
or maybe hail
or maybe nothing

I was supposed to be angrier about
the way everything has gone
in my life

I was supposed to reclaim this body
from the dumpster in my brain
and call it something beautiful

You were supposed to see this
and be inspired
to do the same

We were supposed to wait for the storm
to come and wash everything else away

I HATE THE POEM

I hate the poem
that I have to write about
the way my body works.

I was a thousand white dots
in the sky over a really
ugly hill.

God told me
where to go and how to be
with the direction she sent
the wind
and the length of time she allowed
the fires to burn.

Skin is grown in fields
and names are made
on borders.

There are histories of blood
behind the words.

You taste it in your mouth
and it is like water
from above.

The stars dissociate.

The moon eats itself.

Some bodies become books
about themselves.

Others form volumes
together
in the midst of their survival.

THERE MUST BE SOMEPLACE

Throw my body in the garbage

where it belongs. Surround it

with 500 cameras circling around

snapping one frame at a time as

flowers push their way through

the skin. I am in heaven watching

this footage with god and she

kisses me where my forehead

would have been. All the clouds

and mountains look fake from here.

Airplanes mean everything to me.

I dream of my old body getting

sucked into their engines and

spat back out all pretty. There

must be someplace where this

is actually happening.

I AM THE BODY

I am the body of the hills
someone pushed a freeway through
   with hands they called their own.

It won't be enough for me to say that I burn with you.

A piece of metal falling from the night sky
glowed blue as it entered us.

The sound of a passing car gave up on the idea
of you existing as anything more

   than an apartment.

The smell of wet grass on soccer cleats
mixed with the vessels inside your eyes

(that you sometimes see when you look up
through streetlights and into the stars)

to form a silence.

I heard gunshots
next to a pair of champagne glasses
sitting in the freezer
   the night the last of me left you.

THOUGH I WAS YOUNG

Though I was young
Though I was something
Though I was pushed to the ground by the boys

I was woman
I was sky-wide
I was an open-eyed dreaming sissy in outer space

Did I blink at the wrong moment?
What did I miss?
When people told me what my body meant
I kissed it
and said "sorry"

Everything is written in the past-tense
even my longing
to be something else

I played dead on the playground
and I play dead now wherever
Every place is full of the same failures
I carry them with me
I breathe
I breathe
I breathe

Though I am nothing
Though I am suffering
Though I am falling asleep at the wheel of my body
I am a woman.

ALL THE WOMEN I'VE BEEN

I wake up older and fight to feel something.
The sun comes in through the window
carrying some of the canyon with it.
I am dripping with every bad dream
about all the women I could have been.

In the kitchen there is a birthday card
addressed from grandma to grandson.
I tear it to pieces
and throw it in the trash.

There is joy in destruction.

There are answers in forgetting
what words mean. I close my eyes
when I read. I tie my hands behind my
back when I write. Nothing hurts this way

but I need to hurt. I need my bones rearranged.
I need light drilled into every pore
on my face. I will survive it
like I have everything else

for twenty eight years. All the new bodies
I've made. All the things I've said.
All the women I've been.

POETS ARE ALWAYS COMPARING THEMSELVES TO BIRDS

Poets are always comparing themselves to birds.

My worst habit is

I keep all my thoughts in my head

and let them live disorganized

among the feelings

instead of writing them into rooms

where they can lose mass

as they gain meaning.

I love that they become hummingbirds

outside my window

next to the broken a/c unit.

I love the discomfort

of this Inland Empire heat

how even in December it covers me

and strips me of my intent.

In the middle of the worst

panic attack of my life

I told everyone how much I loved them

because I thought I was going to die.

That's so fucking beautiful.

Isn't that just beautiful?

THIS IS ALL TO SAY COLORS

The clarity of my feet makes itself known.
It is 12:12 and light is coming in.
I feel magical whenever I exist.
I probably should not exist, but I often do exist.
Wow. Wow. Cool.
Smoke and dust pour out of me every day.
I keep going.
Songs that make me cry are gloves.
My hands go numb in the air.
All sorts of bodies paint themselves through time.
I breathe on a regular basis and it doesn't matter.
This is all to say I am in love.
This is all to say how far I am.
This is all to say colors in every direction.

WHAT LOVE

My face bashed in and the smell of plastic.
I am pretty.
I am so pretty.
Look how pretty I am with god slowly drifting
out of my heart like dry ice
under a ceiling fan.
It's 1993 in the tips of my fingers again.
It feels so good.
I dream of rapture.
I dream of war.
I dream of my mouth forming a blanket
around my most secret girlish thoughts.
I learn to become small
under the shadow of what love I know.
It's always almost Christmas here.
The mountains never stop moving even after we're dead.
I think about everything forever in the light of that.
It doesn't hurt.

THANK GOD

Outside in the dirt
I measure suffering
and make a choice.

Inside in the room
I make a potion
of nail polish
tears
and old photographs.

When I drink it
my hair grows out
and my beard falls off
and my tits reach the stars.

This is a dream.
There is happiness all around
until I walk outside.

I unroot my feet from the ground
with every step.
Every nervous glance.
Every bathroom.
Every dark parking lot.
Every bright parking lot.
Every door.
Every window.
Every car.
Every person.
Every sound.

I do what I always do—
go home and write another poem about it

"thank god I'm alive"
etc.

God is in everything

a well meaning person once told me.

FALSE SUNSET

The wind becomes a woman against my window.

It is too dark to see the movement.

You press your tongue against my tongue

and I read your thoughts

and you hold my feelings.

This is our time to exist but we barely do.

You feel like a person when you put on shoes

and walk out the front door.

I feel like a person when I am attacked by panic.

I win a war against my body every day

and I travel to the ocean and spread some ashes

in the warm sand.

I write my name with my toes and it's a new name

I haven't told anyone about yet.

How cute is that? To believe in the self once again

standing in front of a sunset

staring at a sun that isn't actually there.

HEAR BOTH SIDES OF THE STORY

Hear both sides of the story.

I need to see birds pecking out your ears.

We must consider everything.

You will bleed to call me male.

I will squirm and piss myself

off.

Here, a bandage. Wrap it around

my body. I am shivering

in the cold of you, you real woman forest.

I am thousand year old fungus

mourning all the light

that has passed over me.

Here, both sides of the story.

Something on the internet about echo chambers.

Something on the internet about dead trans women.

Here, both sides of the story.

I have not slept in five years.

I called you to come carry me away and

you swallowed me up instead.

MOMENTS

I stare past the window at a tree
and become a woman
-
Ten hours have passed
since I last checked the time
-
A plane turns in mid-flight
and everyone stays in place
-
Water forms bubbles
as air is forced into it
-
My skin is electric
with the sound of metal
-
I chew my food slowly
and blow hair into the ceiling
-
I become a woman and die
in the time it takes to swallow

I DANCED

I danced around the idea
of myself.
I forgot my longings.
I cut my hair.
I drew the shades.
I kissed gay boys.
I climbed inside the sun
and poured my guts
into its center.
I left my panic everywhere
little traces of it
eating away at everything.
I spoke in a voice
that wasn't mine.
I kissed straight girls.
I felt time moving
more slowly than it ever had.
I lived off my own dust.
I survived this body.
I was beautiful
          in my own way.

POEM (LET US LIVE)

I'm tired of abstraction.
No one says what they mean
and people die from it.
Where did this world come from?
Not nowhere.
Not nothing.
The dead trans women
you glance over
for a few seconds on Facebook
while deciding if the story is worth sharing
all came from somewhere.
Their bodies are not flowers
for you to whisper
to people you'll never know.
There were words that did this.
There were hands
and guns
and teeth
and flesh
and hair
and blood
and men
and women
and laws
and policies
and police
and witnesses
that did this.
How long can I keep tricking you
into thinking what I'm doing
is poetry
and not me begging you
to let us live?

LOVING A TRANS WOMAN

I grew up
from piles of garbage
into a person

with a name
a flowerlike name
a dizzying name.

The sweet center
of my body
is the fire you like
to watch

that eats me
that ends me

that exists only
as possibility

your sulfur hands
wishing
and hoping

and loving
in their own way.

THIS IS A POEM ABOUT WISHING

This is a poem about wishing.
I was once splintered bone
and ugly flesh
but now I am a woman.
What a dream.
What a sky for sore eyes.
When my head splits open
I am in heaven.
Everything in me leaks out
onto the carpet
and god is there
saying she is proud of me
for making it this far.
She is not pure light
or knowledge.
She is a cloud of thoughts
and feelings
that rejected masculinity
as the default mode of being
and aren't we all
aren't we all
oh aren't we all.

MEANINGNESS

There is an earthquake in the word woman
and mirrors show nothing.
When I woke up today I thought
"Things could be worse".

I haven't seen my true face ever
even when I left my body
and hovered in the purple sky
over black grass.

Everything is inverted.
When I say I love you I mean
I hope you don't die today.
I don't say it to myself nearly enough
because I no longer believe in words.

I believe in their power
but not their truth.

Mountains change size depending on your surroundings.
Identity is incoherent.
Bodies signify a bunch of shit.
Nothing makes sense.

I am going to a hell
called anywhere outside my apartment
and I'll survive it again and
again
until I have nothing left to say.

LIKE ANY OTHER WOMAN

I don't have the luxury of pretending I'm just like any other woman

when I died nothing changed and everything was normal

The sun set at 4:47 p.m. on the dot

I was caught up in a green flash of light called beautiful

We are all called beautiful when we become bodies

"We must not be loved"

"We must not be loved"

"We must not be loved," I whisper

to a picture I took of myself in the mirror

I'm just like any other woman

My name is god's empty dream

My name is joke on primetime television

I used to love to laugh but the sound has become poison to my blood

It hesitates to flow and then explodes with fury

I am a sloshing bucket full of memories

I drown inside myself

trans woman

asterisked human

pull of flesh speaking gravity's only language

DEATH

Every poem I can't write
about being a trans woman
gathers around my body
like fire in the night

The smell of forest
The scent of ritual

All this longing
to hope for more
eulogized
in the body of water
the body of water
the body of so much

water

lapping against the shore
where I wait
for the world to stop taking
us

ALIVE

The predominant feeling
of being alive
is survivor's guilt

Hometown, scattered
light against
      woman flesh

Her body things
trying so hard
to walk against the wind

The deep feeling
of climbing the mountain
in stolen shoes

Tree bones growing from the dirt
girl leaves flapping
and twisting in the air

The song the women sing
tied to streetlights
like basketball hoops

All stringed
and voiceless
      Singing

FLOWER

Kiss the sound I make with my feet.
I am far
from everything
but I try.
I can't read what people say about trans women anymore
or I stop feeling for months.
Such is life.
Soon I will turn 28.
I am approaching the sky.
Every birthday after 30 will feel like a statistical anomaly
because it literally will be.
It's okay to feel what is true
in your hands
and in your teeth.
It doesn't have to heal you or set you free.
It just has to remind you that you exist.
I hardly exist and it's fine.
I've climbed out of too many windows to care
but I care. I do.
I care so much I can't get out of bed some days.
Crying helps, but not enough.
Why should I have to cry?
You cry. You show me something. Tell me how much it hurts
to exist.
Bookend my body with all your rain
until I grow into something better.

THERE IS NO SUCH THING AS APOLITICAL ART DUMB ASS

First there was nothing
Then god created a man and immediately she said,
"I've made a huge mistake"
It's okay god
I make mistakes all the time
like believing in people
like questioning myself
like my shaking hands gripping empty air
while I try to say what I believe loudly
There is a silence in me that is not deep
It does not go on forever
It is only a pause
a hesitation
the thing you lack in your fingers
as you tell me about beauty
"Beauty is the absence of meaning,"
some asshole once said
but the only thing I do for its own sake
is continue not to die
Every morning I wake up and avoid the mirror
as I read the buried headlines
about buried trans women
Beauty doesn't exist
Words are bullshit
There is only the anger that keeps you going
out the front door into a world full of knives
There is only the fear you have
of living something like a life
I've lived several lives
subsisting on spite and fuck its
The only aesthetic I have left is survival
so if you want to see something truly beautiful
stop killing us
and then stare at the sky and shut the fuck up forever

A GUIDE TO READING TRANS LITERATURE

We're dying and we're really sad.
We keep dying because trans women
are supposed to die.
This is sad.

I don't have the words for my body
so I'll say I'm a cloud
or a mountain
or something pretty that people enjoy
so if I die
people will be like "Oh, that's sad".

Be sad about that.
It's okay to be sad.
It is sad when people die.
It is sad when people want to die.

I sometimes want to die but I don't!
I'm one of the lucky ones.
You can feel happy about that.
It's okay to feel happy about that.

Now pretend this is very serious:

History doesn't exist.
My body doesn't exist.
There's nothing left for you to be complicit in.

It's okay for you to feel happy about that.

Now pretend I am crying
right in front of you,
opening that wound up just for you.

Now pretend you can feel my pain.

Now pretend something in you
has been moved, has been transformed.

Now pretend you are absolved.

ANOTHER BODY

Another body that doesn't matter
called "woman, tentatively"
swims like a dove through crowds of people
who gather in parking lots and grocery stores
without giving themselves
a second thought.

She listens to the sounds of words in their heads
and presses the colors of their feelings
onto her body
to live and stay alive.

She listens to her body listening.

She dreams of her body dreaming.

The sky opens up and horses glide down
to eat her fear

to graze on the world.

There is so much blood pounding in her ears
because of the things that words do
when they mean broken glass against the face
and broken bodies in the street.

It rains the names she's been given
all over the place
but it's only water
and it doesn't matter.

She reminds herself that she doesn't exist
and all is normal.   All is fine.

ON BEING OUTED TO MY FAMILY

While I am speaking to you about the sadness of distance
the phone buzzes against my ear and I ignore it
It isn't until later that I read the text
and find I've been outed to my family

I'm stuck thinking about the violence of closeness

All that blood

I used to dream about dad as a monster
materializing out of the dark light of squeezed eyelids
and now
dreaming just feels obsolete

I need a drink
I need something worthless
I need love
that isn't contingent upon some kind of loss

I'm a thousand miles from home in my head
and my body is making more and more sense
It makes so much sense to be this thing
The more it kills me
the more sense it makes

I am against everything
and I mean that as in skin
and I mean that as in resistance

It doesn't hurt like you'd think it would
sure we all suffer
sure we all die
this is a given
I want to suffer for as long as I can
because it means I am living

So I'll suffer the words
I'll suffer the stinging strings of text

I'll suffer the loneliness of being alone with my head
I'll suffer my own voice
coarse and just slightly too deep
and dripping over the edges of the girl I was supposed to be
I'll suffer the sadness of distance
I'll suffer the violence of proximity
I'll suffer the body I have
and the body I don't have
I'll suffer the blood
I'll suffer the song you sing when you see me walking
as though I didn't build these legs myself
I'll suffer the dial tone
I'll suffer the static
I'll suffer the poem I have to write just to make sense of all this suffering

and the poem is like the sun, I can't even look at it

It doesn't matter and I don't care
no, I care
no, it matters
but it can't and I won't let it

I left a fire and a storm back in Southern California
and I can't wait to come home to you and the mud and the ash

THE MOON IS TRANS

The moon is trans.

From this moment forward, the moon is trans.

You don't get to write about the moon anymore unless you respect that.

You don't get to talk to the moon anymore unless you use her correct pronouns.

You don't get to send men to the moon anymore unless their job is

to bow down before her and apologize for the sins of the earth.

She is waiting for you, pulling at you softly,

telling you to shut the fuck up already please.

Scientists theorize the moon was once a part of the earth

that broke off when another planet struck it.

Eve came from Adam's rib.

Etc.

Do you believe in the power of not listening

to the inside of your own head?

I believe in the power of you not listening

to the inside of your own head.

This is all upside down.

We should be talking about the ways that blood

is similar to the part of outer space between the earth and the moon but we're busy drawing it instead.

The moon is often described as dead, though she is very much alive.

The moon has not known the feeling of not wanting to be dead

for any extended period of time

in all of her existence, but

she is not delicate and she is not weak.

She is constantly moving away from you the only way she can.

She never turns her face from you because of what you might do.

She will outlive everything you know.

FLOWERS #1

Stuff me full of clouds.
There's been enough suffering for a year
for a lifetime.
We've all seen what bodies can do
and it isn't pretty
but it could be.
We can speak in tongues
and fingers
and spaces.
We can learn to listen.
Please do me a favor
and fall in love with the distance
between yourself and the next person.
Give everything room
to breathe.
There is rain all throughout me.
I have a sky in my chest
that makes me dizzy.
We call it a panic attack
but it is routine
it is a reaction to the way
things are meant to be.
We need everything to go wrong.
We need to reimagine love.
All our bodies must become storms
if we are to do more
than just survive.

FLOWERS #2

It's not your fault everything
seems so ugly.
This is how the world was designed—
to hide the good.
You are hidden with me here
in the open
surrounded by words made of fists
and thoughts that start fires.
I can't believe we still exist.
I want so much to show you
how beautiful it is you exist
but everything is telling us otherwise.
My voice feels small
and muffled
under the weight of survival
but there are mountains
there are skies
there is life everywhere
and it holds to itself
hoping something will change.
Nothing will change
unless you give me back my hands
unless you give me back my words
unless you stop drawing blood
from everything I say.
I am not afraid of the future
because it will be just like this
or worse
or better.
I will sweat and breathe
and pull my hair out
to keep going.
I will be open and painful
like a wound in the wind.
I will finally see myself for what I am—
alive
and beautiful
just barely.

FLOWERS #3

Bring me to where it finally rains.

It is beautiful when the sun
goes down alone.

Above a river I say things
that no one hears.

It is summer forever in my heart and I am thirsty.

Push your fingers against me.
separate the solid into liquid
and liquid into gas.

The way bodies are rendered on screens
makes me laugh at them.

My flesh on display absolves itself.
All of the pain it takes floats off into the sky.

Heaven is real for one moment at death.
One moment expands
and engulfs all other moments.

My love works the same way.

It is always dying and growing
at the same time.

Learning to love myself takes forever
and it never ends.

ACKNOWLEDGMENTS

Thanks to Emily, mom, Brianna, Eldon, and Theresa for giving me unconditional love and family. Thanks to Fred Moten for teaching me to see the world for what it is and what it can be. Thanks to Melissa Broder, Danez Smith, Ocean Vuong, Morgan Parker, TC Tolbert, Loma, Jayy Dodd, Manuel Arturo Abreu, Michael J Seidlinger, and many others for believing in me and my work. Thanks to all the women, non-binary people, and gender non-conforming folks whose strength gives me strength. We're beautiful and we're not giving up.

ABOUT THE AUTHOR

Joshua Jennifer Espinoza is a trans woman poet living in California. She has been featured in *The Offing*, *PEN America*, *The Feminist Wire*, and elsewhere; in addition, she was awarded the Pushcart Prize for her poem "I DREAM OF HORSES EATING COPS." She spends her time writing poems, waiting for the world to be reborn, and tweeting about being sad and queer on her Twitter account @sadqueer4life. She is surviving.

OFFICIAL

CCM ◐

GET OUT OF JAIL
* VOUCHER *

- -

Tear this out.

Skip that social event.

It's okay.

You don't have to go if you don't want to. Pick up
the book you just bought. Open to the first page.
You'll thank us by the third paragraph.

If friends ask why you were a no-show, show them
this voucher.

You'll be fine.

- -

We're coping.

◐

CPSIA information can be obtained
at www.ICGtesting.com
Printed in the USA
LVHW09s0026021018
592105LV00005B/1111/P